KU-215-600

Karen Wallace

Rockets

Illustrated by Paul Collicutt

OXFORD
UNIVERSITY PRESS

This book belongs to

OXFORD
UNIVERSITY PRESS

Great Clarendon Street, Oxford OX2 6DP

Oxford University Press is a department of the University of Oxford.
It furthers the University's objective of excellence in research, scholarship,
and education by publishing worldwide in

Oxford New York

Athens Auckland Bangkok Bogotá Buenos Aires Calcutta
Cape Town Chennai Dar es Salaam Delhi Florence Hong Kong Istanbul
Karachi Kuala Lumpur Madrid Melbourne Mexico City Mumbai
Nairobi Paris São Paulo Singapore Taipei Tokyo Toronto Warsaw

Oxford is a registered trade mark of Oxford University Press
in the UK and in certain other countries

Text copyright © Karen Wallace 2000
Illustrations copyright © Paul Collicutt 2000

The moral rights of the author and artist have been asserted

First published 2000

All rights reserved.
British Library Cataloguing in Publication Data available

Hardback ISBN 0–19–910612-6
Paperback ISBN 0–19–910613-4
Pack of 6 ISBN 0-19-910757-2
Pack of 36 ISBN 0-19-910758-0

This edition is also available in Oxford Reading Tree
Branch Library Stages 8-10 Pack A

3 5 7 9 10 8 6 4 2

Printed in Spain by Edelvives.

Contents

VROOM!

▶ Rockets are amazing!

Rockets are amazing!
They can fly in space.
They can fly underwater.

They can fly for
thousands of miles
and hit exactly
what they were
aiming for.

Trident

WHOOSH!

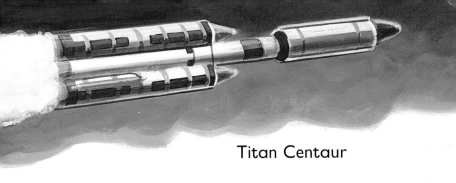

Titan Centaur

KAPOW!

SS 18

BOOM!

▶ How rockets work

How does a rocket work?

Think of a balloon. Blow it up
and let it go. What happens?

WHOOSH!

WHOOSH!

Air escapes through the neck
and the balloon shoots off.

WHOOSH!

VROOM!

Think of a rocket.

Fuel burns inside it and makes gases.

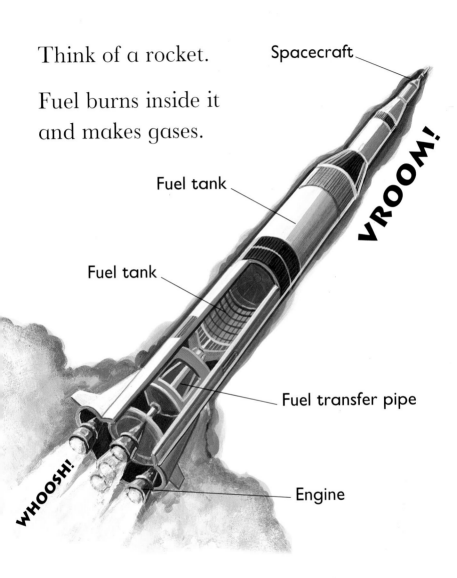

Spacecraft

Fuel tank

Fuel tank

Fuel transfer pipe

Engine

VROOM!

WHOOSH!

WHOOSH! The gases escape through the bottom and **VROOM!** the rocket takes off.

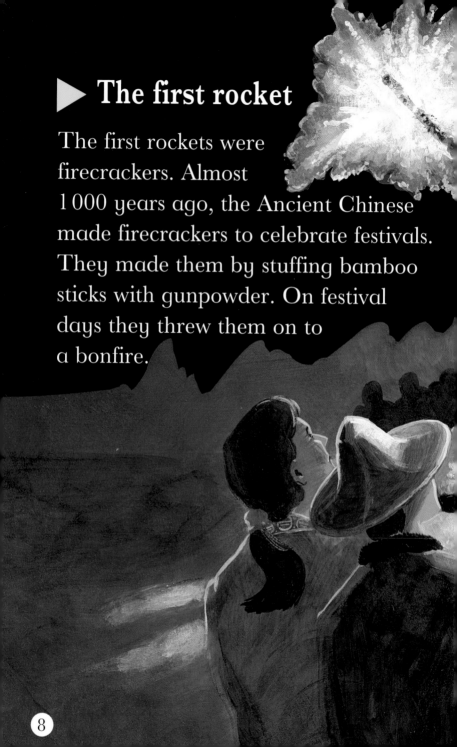

▶ The first rocket

The first rockets were firecrackers. Almost 1000 years ago, the Ancient Chinese made firecrackers to celebrate festivals. They made them by stuffing bamboo sticks with gunpowder. On festival days they threw them on to a bonfire.

Then one day a firecracker flew into the air and exploded. **BANG!**

That firecracker was the first rocket in the world.

The Ancient Chinese soon used their bamboo rockets as weapons. They tied them to arrows and fired them at their enemies. These weapons were called fire arrows. Even the fiercest warriors were terrified.

Over hundreds of years men experimented with rockets. They wanted to invent weapons to win battles.

Did you know...
The Chinese shot thousands of fire arrows against the Mongol invaders and frightened them away.

But there was one big problem.
No one could invent a rocket that
flew straight. Armies fired thousands
and thousands of rockets at each
other but hardly any hit their target.

Then everything changed.

▶ The first modern rocket

In 1926, an American called Robert Goddard built a new kind of rocket.

This new rocket used liquid fuel and it went faster and further than ever before.

It shot up twelve and a half metres, flew for two and a half seconds and landed in a cabbage patch!

Scientists thought it was a great success.

The launch of Goddard's rocket

▶ A World War II rocket

In World War II a German scientist invented a special rocket. For the first time, it could carry a bomb.

This rocket was called the V2.

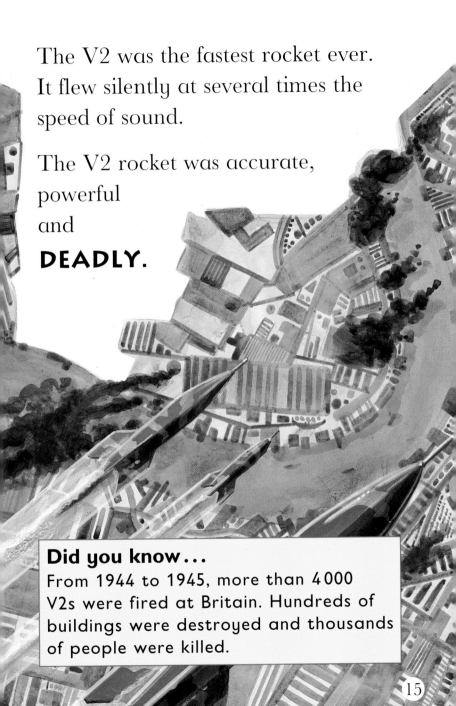

The V2 was the fastest rocket ever. It flew silently at several times the speed of sound.

The V2 rocket was accurate, powerful
and
DEADLY.

Did you know...
From 1944 to 1945, more than 4000 V2s were fired at Britain. Hundreds of buildings were destroyed and thousands of people were killed.

▶ Many kinds of missiles

Rapier
missiles

Today rockets that carry bombs are called missiles. Over the years many different kinds of missiles have been invented.

Some can hit planes in the air.
Some can hit tanks on the ground.
Some can hit ships at sea.

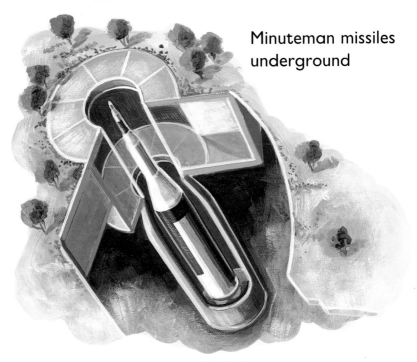

Minuteman missiles underground

Many missiles are hidden underground so they can be fired secretly.

Underwater missiles can be launched from submarines.

But rockets are not only used to carry weapons.

Polaris submarine launches a missile

▶ Man on the moon!

The first rocket to carry a man into space was built by the Russians.

The first rocket to carry a man to the moon was built by the Americans. It was called the Saturn V.

This rocket was as tall as a skyscraper. It carried three astronauts in the Apollo spacecraft.

On July 16, 1969 it took off from the launch pad. It shot off at 25 000 miles per hour.

WHOOSH!

VROOM!

Apollo
spacecraft

Saturn V rocket

Four days later, on 20 July 1969, the most amazing thing happened. Neil Armstrong, the astronaut, climbed out of the spacecraft.

He was the first man to walk on the moon.

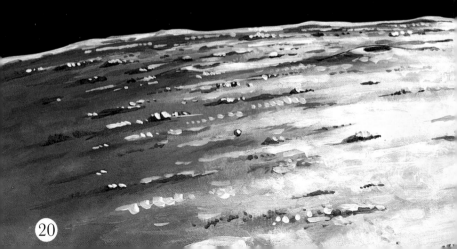

First moon landing

Satellites

▶ Satellites

Rockets still carry astronauts into space but some are built specially to carry space machines called satellites.

There are all kinds of satellites in space.

Some provide extra television programmes and telephone lines.

Ariane 5 rocket with satellites

Others warn us
of bad weather.

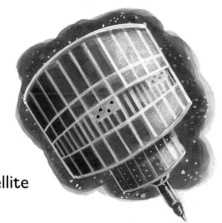

Meteosat
weather satellite

Rockets are also used to carry
satellites that explore space. They
gather information and send it
back to earth.

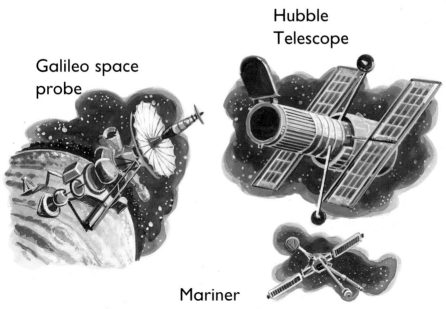

Hubble
Telescope

Galileo space
probe

Mariner
space probe

▶ Space junk

Most rockets that carry satellites are only used once, because the rocket drops away when the satellite is in orbit.

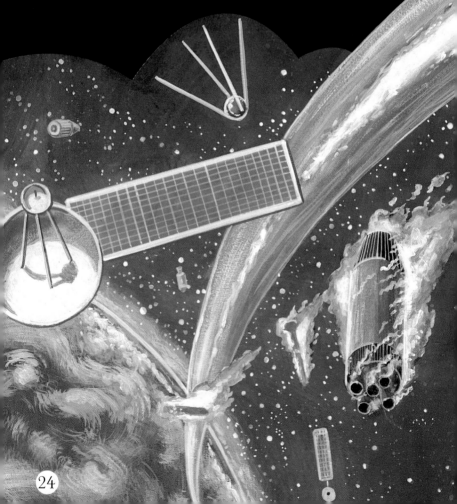

This means old rockets and broken satellites are floating about in outer space.

This is a big problem. Imagine if there was a collision!

So scientists invented a machine that could carry a satellite into space and return to earth.

They called it the space shuttle.

The space shuttle is half rocket, half aeroplane.

It roars into space like a rocket. It flies through space and lands back on earth like an aeroplane.

The space shuttle can be used again and again.

Space shuttle in space

Did you know...
The space shuttle can even bring back broken satellites from outer space.

Space shuttle landing back on earth

▶ Blast Off!

Rockets really are amazing!

Imagine you are a scientist and you are sitting in your own spacecraft. Huge rockets are ready to lift you off the ground.

WHOOSH!

You are going to build
a space station on Mars.

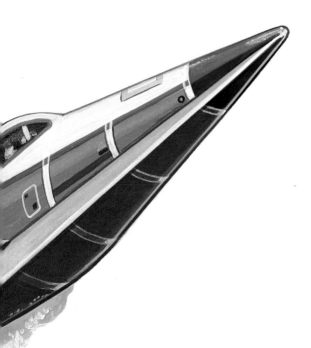

Countdown begins.
5! 4! 3! 2! 1!
The rocket engines **ROAR** ...

BLAST OFF!

Glossary

 gunpowder Gunpowder is a powder which explodes when it is lit.   **8**

 launch pad Rockets take off into space from a platform called the launch pad.   **18**

 liquid fuel Liquid fuel in rockets is oxygen and hydrogen in liquid form. They burn to make power and heat.   **12**

 orbit When something is in orbit it circles round a planet in space.   **24**

 satellite A satellite is a machine that has been sent into space to gather information.   **22, 23, 24, 25, 26**